LEARNING

HOW

TO

RIDE A BIKE

AS AN ADULT

Lessons learnt while navigating uncertainty

...For us

Contents

Acknowledgments 3

Section 1: Prologue 5

Section 2: Introduction 6

Section 3: Lessons 1-10 7

    Lesson 1: Manage your expectations! 7

    Lesson 2: Permission to Play?! 8

    Lesson 3: Keep Your head up! 10

    Lesson 4: Your Story Matters, Tell It! 12

    Lesson 5: Analyze but don't get Paralyzed! 14

    Lesson 6: Trust your Instincts! 16

    Lesson 7: Words Matter, Always Speak Life! 19

    Lesson 8: The Power of Influence! 20

    Lesson 9: The 10,000 hours Concept! 22

    Lesson 10: Principle of Belief! 24

Acknowledgments

A very special thank you to my teacher
'Spicy'

Section 1: Prologue

As a child, I never learned how to ride a bike. When I turned 21, I had the desire to learn but never took the opportunities granted to me to achieve this. In hindsight, I was crippled with a lot of irrelevant fears. Am I too old? Who learns at this age? What if I don't get it? And as time went by, these fears magnified and left me with a dream that I wasn't sure would become a reality.

Last year, I decided enough was enough. How much longer would I let these fears rob me of the things that I want to do? So, I bought a bike and decided that either way, I would prove myself right or wrong, but I would not leave the rest of my life thinking, "what if?"

SECTION 2: INTRODUCTION

WHY WAS LEARNING HOW TO RIDE A BIKE SO IMPORTANT TO ME?

For the last ten years, fitness has been an essential part of my life. In 2019, while I was training for the 2020 Miami Half Marathon, I injured my knee. Running has always been my preferred mode of keeping fit, and I knew that it was only a matter of time until I needed to find an alternative. Life finds a way to bring you back to where you started and gives you another chance to either accept the challenge or fold.

As I started the journey, I began to journal through the process, and slowly things began to seem more profound than the surface. Here, I share a few lessons with you that I picked up along the way.

Section 3: Lessons 1-10

Lesson 1: Manage your expectations!

Day 1- My friends had me so hyped! "This is easy! You can do it in your sleep. You got this. All you need is a few hours. It's really a one-and-done experience!"

I left the park that day frustrated and mortified. My first experience learning how to ride a bike was nothing like I thought it would be. I felt slightly defeated, battling the "what is wrong with me? why couldn't I do it in those few hours?" thoughts that love to pop up at the first sign of adversity.

Nevertheless, I knew that would not be the last time my bike saw me. I needed to change my strategy and return with the right mindset. On this day, I learned not to step into a new field with massive expectations. Receive each part of the process in order to adjust accordingly, make the necessary changes and begin again.

Lesson 2: Permission to Play?!

Ready to get back to it, I recruited one of my besties, a fantastic teacher, to walk me through the rest of the journey. Blessed to have her, she held my hand as I hopped back on the bike at the crowded park to see me pedal at least two revolutions at a go for hours in the hot Miami sun!

To my surprise, most of those who noticed that I was learning, encouraged me to keep on going. It amazed me that when I took some time to reflect at the end of the day, I realized that all who did were of a different race. My fellow black people, avoided all eye contact till I talked to them and casually brought their walls down. It was then and only then that they began sharing openly, giving me advice, and cheering me on.

I was puzzled as to why the other races were comfortable in this exchange while those I expected to recognize me, see me and support me the most weren't. Why were they so comfortable expressing themselves regardless of my feedback or lack thereof while my fellow melanin enriched counterparts waited for a pass?

Was this situation a one-off, or was this yet another subtle reminder of our daily reality? I couldn't help but think of the times that I also had my reservations in similar encounters and wondered how many opportunities to engage, had I also allowed to pass me by.

Lesson 3: Keep Your Head Up!

As I began trying to balance on the bike, I found myself looking down to put both feet on the pedals. This was a significant struggle until a group of ladies on their Sunday Morning bike slowed down and gave me the advice that changed the game. "Make sure you keep your head up, don't look down to put the second foot up. Look up straight, your foot will find its way to the pedal."

Sure enough, they were right. I was able to make the first few pedals after so many failed tries. I couldn't believe it. It went against everything I had assumed I naturally needed to do.

As I thought about it, it was a clear reminder that in general, as we go through life, setbacks are indeed inevitable. Progress can only be made when you look at what is ahead and your focus is centered on the destination.

Your vision and what you see will determine how far you go. Where there's a will you will always find a way. Keep your head up regardless of how heavy it feels.

Lesson 4: Your Story Matters, Tell It!

The next day, we showed up bright and early to beat the midmorning heat. An older woman who seemed to be in her 70s walks by as I struggled to get 3-4 pedals in. She stops and stares at me, saying, "Young lady, I learned how to ride a bike after 30, you know. I grew up on a farm, and I thought it was the most difficult thing at the moment. But If I can do it, anyone can! You can!"

She stood by and waited for me get back on the bike and continued on her journey after cheering me on the bit of progress I had made. Those words meant the world to me at that very moment. Frustration had begun to set in, and I had slowly started drifting into the mental space that over analyzes everything, wondering why one plus one wasn't equating to two.

There is so much power in relativity. Knowing that I was not the first and neither would I be the last to go through this gave me all the confidence I needed for the day. It also had me question all the times that I could have shared my story with others but didn't think that my narrative was minute or mundane. Was I robbing others of the same chance? If I can help it, never again!

Lesson 5: Analyze but Don't Get Paralyzed!

The weekend was over, but the journey had just begun. I needed to find a way to continue working on the progress regardless of how busy the weekdays were.

This particular day was a late one, and the night was setting in. I needed to find a safe place to practice quickly. Feeling the pressure, the session that was supposed to be a fun and exciting one took a scientific approach. I would stop and analyze each error I made, trying to figure out how not to repeat it. This would then result in making the same mistake again or an entirely different one.

Weariness started settling in rapidly, and I stopped. Doubt began to creep in as I began to ask myself "Is this where I get stuck? Is this where it all ends?" Amid the mental chaos, Aaliyah's song "Try Again" started playing through my mind. I embraced her wisdom and kept putting my foot back up on the pedal. I looked up and did it over and over and over again.

That night, I made it from one side of the park to the other pedaling nonstop. I learned then that although the steps may not be perfect, they are still a part of progress.

Lesson 6: Trust your Instincts!

Our gut is one of God's best gifts to man! At this point, I had learned how to let go of the mental scrutiny but was yet to learn how to trust myself. Like the previous ones before, this day had me so nervous about falling and losing my teeth, bruising my skin or worse - breaking a bone.

I was not ready to show off any battle scars and since this could have easily become my reality, I gripped the bike handles forcefully. Terrified, as it was the only thing separating me from the earthy embrace I needed to avoid at all costs. As I started pedaling, I noticed my body shifting to account for the lack of balance.

My body and mind worked together to do all they can to protect me, and all I needed to do was trust. The body, mind, and instincts are our internal compass driving us to success. As long as we listen to them and followed their guidance, we will not be let down.

LESSON 7: WORDS MATTER, ALWAYS SPEAK LIFE!

For me, this was one of the most important lessons. This night, we got to the park, I settled on the bike and was ready to go. Spicy then said the words that completely changed the trajectory of my journey. "Today is the day you ride on your own. You're ready."

I remember hearing these words and internalizing them. This is what I had been waiting for. This was my ***why***. Though I was extremely nervous that it may not happen that day, her belief lessened my unbelief, and I uttered the words, "Okay, I'll try."

I put one foot on the pedal, did the same with the other, and pushed forward. I was wobbling around, anxious but excited, not knowing when or how I would stop. I kept pedaling, embracing each moment, yelling "I'm doing it!". Spicy giggled at my child like excitement while recording the moment so I can have it for life. It was one of the most exhilarating moments I had ever experienced.

Lesson 8: The Power of Influence!

When people around you do things so effortlessly, it is easy for you to believe you can do so as well. I was practicing balance at the park when I saw a little girl, about three years old, learning how to ride a bike. It was a whole family affair, and everyone cheered her on as she tried to pedal and muster up the courage to do it.

When she saw me, her face lit up, and so did mine. We were doing something together! This motivated both of us to keep on going. Despite our differences, that moment bonded us and gave us the courage we both needed. Generally, it is easy for children to see others participate in an activity and not question their ability to do the same.

With adults, we are well aware of the differences between us and others, so it is up to us to seek the extra motivation we need. Finding an online community of others who have done or are attempting to do what you're aspiring to; will provide the support and courage you need to accomplish your goal.

Lesson 9: The 10,000 Hours Concept!

Practice makes progress. The beauty of facing our fears in adulthood is that it makes it clear that fear is just an illusion. As children, we are fearless. As adults, we are more aware of life's unexpected roadblocks that more often than we want, leave us weary. This in turn leads us to develop a skewed outlook that hinders us from realizing our maximum potential.

With this in mind, I took every opportunity to diminish my biggest fears: a) stagnancy during the learning process and b) injury that would hinder the progress. I did this by practicing. I took every opportunity that I had to ride. I rode in the morning, at night, and sometimes twice a day.

Soon, the fear was left behind and I quickly associated riding with fun. This made each practice session very exciting, and I could not wait until the next time I would go out and do it all over again.

Lesson 10:
Principle of Belief!

It only takes one person to believe in you and with you to achieve ANYTHING you want to. As social creatures, the belief or approval from our loved ones can go a mighty long way! You only need one person in your corner to help you get to the finish line.

For some like me, a best friend in their ear cheering them on. For others, it could be spiritual support, or it could be a Youtuber, influencer, or coach that is determined to see you win. Luckily for me, in addition to the in-person support I received, I had all of you reading this right now who encouraged me in different ways and celebrated every win along the way.

It easy to believe that you made it because of your hard work, brilliant work, effort, etc. Although all of these play a role in getting us there, if we carefully look at our journey, we cannot deny that it first begins in our mind. The possibility of knowing that we are capable of making it is what helps us make the first step. No one attempts to do something that they know will end up in failure. The belief that you can is what makes you do!

Thank you for coming on this ride with me!

Love,

gingabibi.